# IMAGES
## *of America*
# FORT PULASKI

IMAGES
*of America*

# FORT PULASKI

John Walker Guss

ARCADIA
PUBLISHING

Published by Arcadia Publishing
Charleston, South Carolina

Printed in the United States of America

Library of Congress Control Number: 2014952753

For all general information, please contact Arcadia Publishing:
Telephone 843-853-2070
Fax 843-853-0044
E-mail sales@arcadiapublishing.com
For customer service and orders:
Toll-Free 1-888-313-2665

Visit us on the Internet at www.arcadiapublishing.com

*I would like to dedicate this book to Talley Kirkland, retired National Park Service historian of Fort Pulaski, and the members of the 48th New York State Volunteer Infantry, Company F, reactivated.*

# CONTENTS

# ACKNOWLEDGMENTS

Fort Pulaski has always drawn me inside its magnificent walls, as a child going on summer vacations with my family, a young man donning a wool uniform as a living historian of the 48th New York State Volunteer Infantry, and then as a professional in the field of historic preservation. Its architecture, like many of the masonry forts across the United States, is a magnificent memorial of grandeur built by our forefathers and heroes. So, perhaps it is only fitting with as much time as I have spent returning to this old fort year after year that I write a story of its remarkable history of development, defense, defeat, and resurrection as one of the nation's premiere national treasures.

As in my previous book *Fortresses of Savannah*, I again would like to give a special thanks to Danny Brown, retired chief ranger of Fort McAllister State Park; Talley Kirkland, retired chief historian of Fort Pulaski National Monument (FPNM); Cullen Chambers, director of the Tybee Lighthouse Museum; and my good friends Marty Liebschner, site manager of Fort James Jackson National Historic Landmark; and previous site manager Greg Starbuck, current executive director at Historic Sandusky.

Finally, a special thanks to current National Park Service rangers Joel Cadoff and Gloria Swift, who assisted me with the viewing and processing of the archives within Fort Pulaski. In addition, Joel's splendid photography helps capture and share the spectacular architecture in this book.

Images credited as (LOC) are courtesy of the Library of Congress. Unless otherwise noted, images are from the author's collection.

# INTRODUCTION

Following the War of 1812 with Great Britain, the United States realized how vulnerable it was against foreign invaders. The capital city of Washington had been burned, its defenses had been challenged, and the US Army did not have a solid foundation to endure another stand up fight against a strong enemy in open field.

Although Pres. Thomas Jefferson and Pres. James Madison had initiated a series of masonry fortifications after the United States had won its independence from England, this "Second System" of masonry forts proved to be quite inadequate, particularly with the acquisition of recent territories and an immediate need to protect them. Under the new leadership of Pres. James Monroe, some $800,000 was allocated to construct a new system of much larger and stronger masonry forts, which would accommodate more cannon and more soldiers.

The primary locations were determined by the strategic coastal waterways and key port cities. Although some 200 locations would be recommended to build new forts, only 42 were approved. From Maine to Louisiana, and ultimately along the California coast, new brick forts began construction from 1816 to 1867. Florida received nine new forts, the most of any state in the country. Many of the Southern states received one to two forts. Georgia only received one, but it would be grand. Fort Pulaski, named in honor of Gen. Casimir Pulaski, who was killed in the assault of the British defenses in the Battle of Savannah on October 9, 1779, was to become one of the more impressive "Third System" brick forts. The primary purpose of this innovative and massive fortification along the coast of Georgia was to protect the Savannah River and the valuable port city of Savannah, originally settled by Gen. James Oglethorpe in 1733.

Oddly enough, all of these innovative forts that had been constructed to defend against foreign invaders never felt any serious threats during their early years of standing watch over the US coastlines. Many of the forts, including Fort Pulaski, experienced a downsizing in staffing of military personnel soon after their construction, and some only had one or two individuals living in them. However, in 1861, the most unpredictable circumstances occurred, with a war raging within the United States. Southern states seceded from the Union, declaring themselves independent, but also demanded that these forts that had been built along their shores come under their custody. Ultimately, the United States would have to destroy and capture the forts it had built to protect itself.

Today, Fort Pulaski is a prominent national monument under the care of the National Park Service. It stands as a memorial to the men and women of the United States who built and defended these mighty fortresses to protect the nation. Thousands of visitors come to the fort each year to learn about the captivating history readers are about to explore here.

In the early 1600s, while North America began to undergo the establishment of settlements by English colonists along its eastern coastlines, potential unknown threats awaited in the interior's wilderness. Leaders of these new settlements included Gen. James Oglethorpe, who spearheaded the colonization of what would become Georgia and authorized the construction of fortifications around the new colony, primarily around the new city of Savannah. These first forts would be built of earth and logs. This sketch by an unknown artist is titled *Building the Fort at Jamestown* (Jamestown, Virginia). (LOC.)

In the early years of Colonial America, the military and citizens built fortifications for defense against the uncertainty of the American Indians, the Spanish, and other potentially unfriendly foes in the interior. When General Oglethorpe arrived on the coast of Georgia, he initiated a series of fortifications on the outer perimeter of the developing city of Savannah. (LOC.)

# One

# THE NEED FOR
# A STRONG DEFENSE

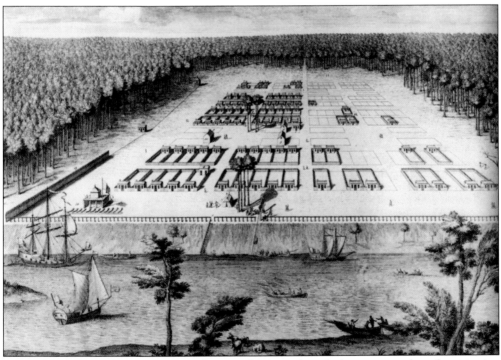

General Oglethorpe began designing the city of Savannah with the strategic plan of positioning this new English settlement on the high bluffs a few miles inland from the ocean, along what would come to be called the Savannah River. He wrote in his report to the trustees in London, "I went myself to view the Savannah River. I fixed upon a healthy situation about ten miles from the sea. The river here forms a half moon, along the south side of which the banks are almost forty foot high and on top flat, which they call a bluff." In addition to building the city along the bluffs, Oglethorpe designed a system of squares, which were quite beautiful, but could also serve as a defensive position in the event of attack. (LOC.)

One of the first documented forts constructed at the mouth of the Savannah River was Fort George, named in honor of King George. In 1761, John Gerar William de Brahm, surveyor general of the Southern District of North America, began designing a fort on Cockspur Island. De Brahm noted that Fort George would be constructed with a small embrasure redoubt 100 feet square, with a blockhouse or bastion 40 feet square and 30 feet high. It would serve as a blockhouse, powder magazine, and barracks for up to 50 British soldiers and have an armament of 11 cannon and 4 mortars. Unfortunately, Fort George was poorly maintained and considered a total ruin by 1772. Just one officer and three enlisted soldiers were left to serve as an outpost. In 1776, during the American Revolution, the cannon were retrieved by American forces and brought into the fortifications of Savannah to defend against the British. Nothing remains of Fort George. This watercolor was painted in December 1764 by W.J. DeRenne.

By 1775, the new American colonies were frustrated with the overbearing rule of King George and the tax mandates that had been forced on the once law-abiding British citizens. The War of American Independence rippled throughout America on April 19, 1775, with the battles at Lexington and Concord, Massachusetts, and every colony soon became a battlefront. The patriots had little success in holding their key cities and were forced to fight on the battlefields and in the woods where they could gain some advantage. The forts and blockhouses, which had been built to defend these colonies in their early development, quickly fell to the powerful British armies.

In 1778, the British army, under the command of Gen. Augustine Prevost, moved into Savannah and the outer defenses, quartering in the townships of Ebenezer to the north and Sunbury to the south. They began reinforcing their positions in preparation of an attack by American and French forces.

## CAPTURE OF SAVANNAH
## DECEMBER 29, 1778

When the British attacked Savannah on December 29, 1778, the defending Continental forces, numbering about 650 men under command of Maj. Gen. Robert Howe, were posted across Sea Island Road (now Wheaton Street) approximately 100 yards east of this marker.

The British army, 2500 strong, landed near Brewton Hill at daybreak on Dec. 29. It consisted of part of the 71st Highland Regt., New York Loyalists, and Hessians, and was commanded by Lt. Col. Archibald Campbell. The British promptly marched on Savannah. They halted on the road about 800 yards from the American battle line and deployed for attack.

Col. Campbell meanwhile learned of an unguarded pass through the swamp, which led around the right of the American line. He there upon detached the Light Infantry under Sir James Baird in an attempt, which proved successful, to flank the Continental position here.

Outflanked, the American position became untenable and Gen. Howe ordered Savannah evacuated. During the withdrawal, the Georgia Brigade, commanded by Gen. Lachlan McIntosh, was cut off and suffered heavy casualties.

During the subsequent siege of Savannah by the French and Americans in 1779 the British line of defenses around the Town ran through this area.

On December 29, 1778, more than 2,500 British troops under the command of Lt. Col. Archibald Campbell landed east of Savannah near Brewton Hill and marched toward the heavily defended American works commanded by Maj. Gen. Robert Howe. The fighting was fierce, and the key to the battle came later when a slave from Sir James Wright's plantation directed Campbell's light infantry along an unguarded road that flanked the American position on the right. The battle turned into a rout, and the Americans were forced to evacuate Savannah. In his journal, Campbell wrote that American casualties included 83 dead, with 38 officers and 415 non-commissioned officers and privates taken prisoner.

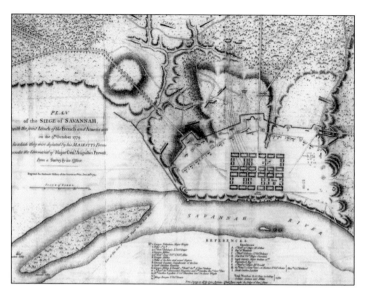

A British officer drew this detailed map of the siege lines of American and French forces and the defensive position of the British forces during the Battle of Savannah on October 9, 1779. Although the American and French forces were far superior in number, totaling more than 5,000 to the British defenders who numbered some 3,200, the British were heavily fortified in earthen defenses. (LOC.)

On October 9, 1779, during the Second Battle of Savannah, combined American and French forces made an attempt at recapturing the city. The fighting was intense as the Americans and French coordinated assaults on the British defenses, particularly at what was known as the Spring Hill Redoubt. Heavy casualties were sustained by the allied forces, which totaled some 948 killed and wounded, while the British army incurred just 155 casualties. It would become known as the second bloodiest battle of the American Revolution. This splendid painting by artist Arthur I. Keller depicts the brutal fighting during the Battle of Savannah. (LOC.)

Maj. Gen. Augustine Prevost took over command of the British forces during the siege of Savannah on January 17, 1779. He had previously served in the Seven Years War and had been given the nickname of "Old Bullet Head" by his men due to a head wound he had sustained in the Battle of Quebec in 1759. During the Battle of Savannah, Prevost had been able to delay the Allied attack long enough to gain reinforcements from Charleston, which may have made the difference in the British victory on October 9, 1779. (LOC.)

Maj. Gen. Benjamin Lincoln was in command of the American forces during the Siege of Savannah in the fall of 1779. Although he was part of the Continental defeat and was later captured in the defense of Charleston, South Carolina, General Washington would give him the distinguished honor of accepting the surrender of the British armies at the Battle of Yorktown in October 1781.

Count Charles Henri-Hector Theodat D'Estaing (1729–1794) commanded 4,000 French troops that reinforced the American offensive, making this the first joint military effort by the United States and France. D'Estaing delivered a demand to General Prevost stating, "In the name of the Most Christian Majesty, Louis XVI, you are summoned to surrender your forces." Prevost rejected the terms, and while the Allied forces failed to coordinate an immediate attack, British reinforcements arrived from Charleston. Having suffered more than 900 casualties and being wounded twice himself, D'Estaing ordered the withdrawal, failing to recapture Savannah.

Sgt. William Jasper, 2nd South Carolina Infantry, distinguished himself in the defense of Charleston when British artillery shot the flagstaff from Fort Moultrie. Jasper climbed the broken flagstaff to remount the colors. For his bravery, Governor Rutledge presented him an officer's commission and sword. However, he humbly declined the promotion, feeling unqualified because of his illiteracy. During the Siege of Savannah, Jasper stormed the Spring Hill Redoubt with fellow soldiers only to be shot down while trying to plant his regiment's colors on the parapet. He was buried in an unidentified mass grave west of Savannah. This illustration from an 1860 edition of *Harper's Weekly* depicts Sergeant Jasper in his heroic act. (LOC.)

Count Casimir Pulaski came to America, inspired by Benjamin Franklin, who was desperately seeking military leaders for the American cause. Pulaski, who had been exiled from his native land of Poland, was granted a commission by General Washington. After displaying extraordinary leadership at the Battle of Brandywine in 1777, Washington promoted him to the rank of brigadier general and gave him command of the cavalry. General Pulaski raised a cavalry regiment in Maryland, which would become known as Pulaski's Legion. In 1779, his legion joined Gen. Benjamin Lincoln in a plan to recapture Savannah. (FPNM.)

This is another portrait of Gen. Casimir Pulaski, painted by artist Julian Rys about 1897. Pulaski later became general of the American cavalry and soldier for American Independence. In his first correspondence to General Washington, Pulaski wrote, "I came here, where freedom is being defended, to serve it, and to live or die for it." (LOC.)

General Pulaski and his cavalry charged through a hail of intense musket and cannon fire toward the Spring Hill Redoubt, a key point of the British defenses. Pulaski was hit by grapeshot in his inner thigh during the assault, and the wounds proved to be deadly. He was carried from the battlefield and put on board the warship *Wasp*, where he soon died. Following his heroic death, Pulaski became known as "The Father of the American Cavalry." (LOC.)

This magnificent monument, which stands in Savannah's Monterey Square, was constructed in 1854 to honor this American hero. Some contemporary historians once believed that Pulaski's body had been entombed underneath the monument. However, most experts agree that when he died on board the *Wasp*, his body was buried in the Atlantic Ocean. Cities, libraries, parks, schools, and streets all across the United States have been named in his honor. One of the most noted memorials named in honor of Casimir Pulaski was Fort Pulaski.

While forts were being suggested and designed along the coastlines of the United States, just three miles east of Savannah, along the Savannah River, Salters Island was chosen as a strategic location for a new masonry fort. It was named in honor of James Jackson, Revolutionary War hero and later governor of Georgia. This early sketch depicts how Fort James Jackson looked to an individual sailing along the Savannah River. (LOC.)

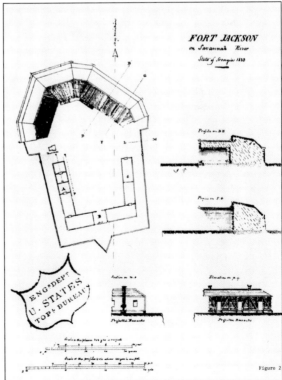

This is a view of some of the original architectural blueprints of Fort James Jackson, dated 1823. Included in these drawings are barracks for the garrison. The original barracks were constructed of wood and then later improved, becoming brick structures. These barracks remained until December 20, 1864, when upon their evacuation, the Confederates set fire to the buildings. Only the foundation of the barracks remains today. (LOC.)

The War of 1812 brought another serious threat to the United States with the burning of Washington, DC, and the testing of some of these new masonry forts, particularly Fort McHenry in Baltimore Harbor, Maryland. They withstood the test of the British might with limited satisfaction. (LOC.)

Savannah had become an important port city of the Southern states and needed to be defended from potential invaders. The city was spared due only to the fact that the War of 1812 ended before British warships could sail up the Savannah River and destroy it. Fort Wayne, Fort Jackson, and other minimal defenses were all that stood in the way of any invading force, and that was not enough. (LOC.)

# Two

# NEW FORTS TO DEFEND AMERICA

Following the War of 1812, Pres. James Madison and others realized there was a dire need for stronger defenses along the coastlines of the adolescent United States. On November 16, 1816, with the support of Secretary of State James Monroe, President Madison authorized Gen. Simon Bernard, former aide-de-camp of Napoleon Bonaparte, to be an assistant in the corps of engineers of the United States. He was promoted to the rank of brigadier general by brevet and given the compensation allowed to the chief of the newly established corps. (LOC.)

Gen. Simon Bernard, former aide-de-camp to Emperor Napoleon I in France, banished by King Louis XVIII following the Hundred Days War, became highly sought after for his expertise in military engineering. On November 16, 1816, President Madison appointed Bernard assistant engineer with the pay and emoluments of a brigadier general. He would become part of a board of officers, which included Maj. (Brevet Colonel) William McRee (McRae) and Maj. (Brevet Lieutenant Colonel) Joseph G. Totten of the US Army; and Capt. J.D. Elliott of the US Navy. They would formulate a strategic plan to build a series of brick fortifications along the US coastline. (LOC.)

Brig. Gen. Joseph G. Totten, a graduate of the US Military Academy at West Point, was one of just three cadets in the class of 1805. He served in the War of 1812, the Mexican-American War, and the Civil War. Totten was involved in overseeing the construction of the Third System of fortifications built along the American coastlines and harbors, which included Fort Williams and Fort Clinton in New York and Fort Adams in Rhode Island. He would become the chief engineer of the US Army in 1838, serving in that position until his death in 1864. Totten would be the longest serving of any chief engineer in US military history. (LOC.)

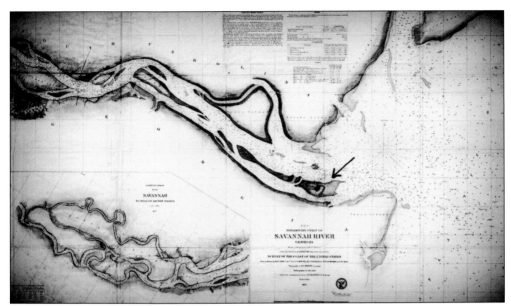

In March 1821, Cockspur Island was chosen as the most strategic point to build this new Third System fortification along the Georgia coast. The fort would be positioned just inside the mouth of the Savannah River to intercept attackers before they entered the main body of the river and made a serious threat on Savannah. The location coordinates were 32 degrees, 2 minutes north latitude, and 3 degrees, 51 minutes west longitude from Washington. The island was considered wholly marsh and measured about a mile long and a half mile wide. This 1855 map shows the location of Fort Pulaski as noted by the arrow. (FPNM.)

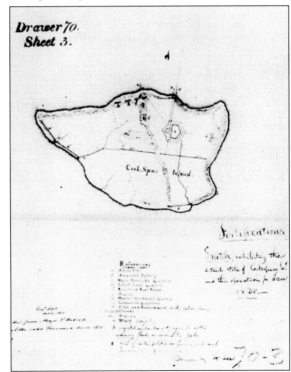

This official map drawn by Lt. Robert E. Lee in January 1830 shows Cockspur Island and the position of the construction of Fort Pulaski. By 1833, the new masonry fortification was still not finished. Weather, funding, and logistics had prolonged the monumental project. (FPNM.)

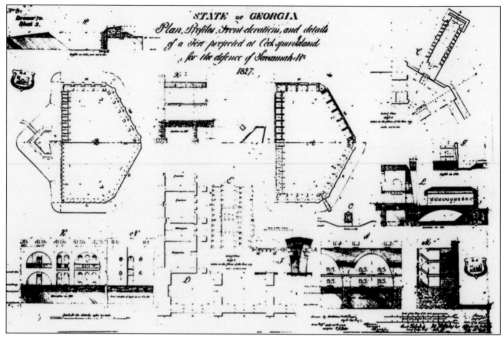

Fort Pulaski was designed to accommodate about one company of 300 soldiers during peacetime and about 800 in time of war. Approximately 150 guns would be implemented to defend the walls. These plans, drawn in 1827, took two years to be prepared before construction could begin. (FPNM.)

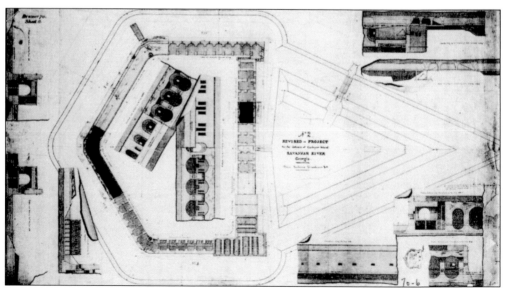

This is another blueprint that shows greater details in the specifications of Fort Pulaski. (FPNM.)

Shown here are the original blueprints of the proposed main entrance or sally port and drawbridge of Fort Pulaski. Reports mention yellow pine, dogwood, and oak as being some of the various woods used in the construction of the fort. Metal materials included iron bolts, nails, spikes, and sheets of copper. (FPNM.)

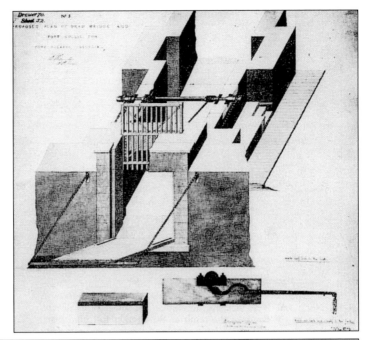

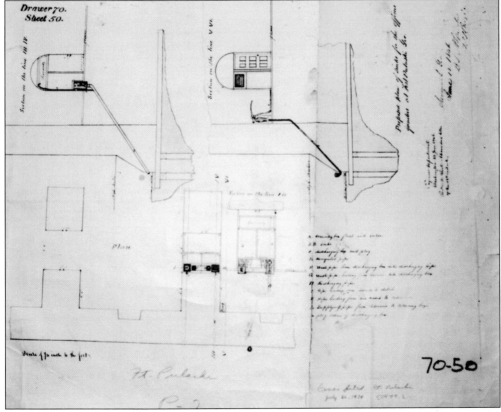

These are the proposed plans of the sinks or restroom facilities for the officer quarters inside the fort. (FPNM.)

Cockspur Island was frequently muddy, with constant flooding and infestations of mosquitoes, alligators, snakes, and other menacing hindrances, which the soldiers and civilians had to endure while building Fort Pulaski. These sketches of an alligator and turtle were drawn by then-lieutenant Robert E. Lee. (FPNM.)

Maj. Samuel Babcock, West Point graduate and veteran of the Mexican-American War, was given command of the construction of Fort Pulaski in 1828. He had previously designed and supervised three other works: Fort McHenry, Fort Covington, and Fort Lookout, as well as one fort named in his honor. He fought in the Battle of Fort McHenry during the War of 1812. Babcock was forced to leave Cockspur Island due to chronic illness believed to have been caused by the severe heat, malnutrition, and constant attacks of mosquitoes. Regrettably, he resigned his commission on December 22, 1830, and returned home to Connecticut, where he died on June 26, 1831. Lt. Joseph King Fenno Mansfield, shown here, was also from Connecticut and a graduate of West Point. He took the place of Major Babcock, was appointed chief engineer in January 1830, and served more than a decade overseeing the construction of Fort Pulaski with the assistance of his subordinate officer, Lt. Robert E. Lee. (FPNM.)

Following the completion of the fort, Mansfield continued his military service, rising to the rank of general in the US Army, serving as a field officer rather than an engineer. In September 1862, at the Battle of Antietam, Maryland, he was on the opposite end of the battlefield from his former fellow officer, now Gen. Robert E. Lee. Mansfield was killed while leading his troops near "The Cornfield." (LOC.)

Accompanying Lieutenant Mansfield to his military assignment at the Fort Pulaski project was another officer of West Point, 2nd Lt. Robert E. Lee. At 23 years of age, he was given his first assignment on September 27, 1829, to join the engineers on Cockspur Island. There, Lee would assist in the design, construction, and engineering of the new fort. He oversaw the repair of the embankments and drainage systems and was later promoted to acting assistant commissary of subsistence of the post. In 1861, Lee would return to Fort Pulaski in a uniform representing a different nation. (FPNM.)

As far back as the 1500s, enslaved Africans were used as a labor force in Africa to build stone fortresses, which are visible today along the continent's coastlines. When the slave trade began to thrive in the United States, the government used enslaved African Americans to help build its defenses. Many were general laborers, but some were skilled craftsmen. (LOC.)

Prior to the Civil War, enslaved African Americans were used as part of the labor force in construction projects throughout the United States. The US military used enslaved African Americans to build Fort Pulaski. However, according to reports by Major Babcock dated June 1830, there were "70 negroes paid at $12 per month." The money may have gone to a potential owner of these African Americans. There was also mention of 15 white men paid $15 per month. (LOC.)

The Hermitage Plantation, owned by Henry McAlpin, was built in the 1820s just a few miles outside of Savannah. The US government contracted McAlpin to produce millions of bricks known as "Savannah Grays." They were manufactured by the enslaved African Americans and paid laborers for the purpose of constructing Fort Pulaski. (LOC.)

These African Americans pose in front of the brick homes in which hundreds of enslaved people lived on the Hermitage Plantation. They were part of the workforce that produced the mass numbers of bricks that went into the construction of Fort Pulaski and other brick structures in the Savannah area. (LOC.)

The archway supports for forts like Fort Pulaski were a spectacular engineering feat. Originally the walls were unpainted, but when the US Army moved into the fort, it painted the walls white, believing it would help contain the moisture and prevent diseases such as malaria and yellow fever. The paint on the walls remains clearly evident today.

This was one of 10 cisterns designed for the inside of the fort to supply the garrison with fresh water. Collectively they could hold up to 200,000 gallons of water. Rain falling on the terreplein would filter through pipes in the walls into the cistern. When the fort fell in April 1862, Union troops added a steam condenser to filter the salt water from the moat into fresh water.

The framework of the main entrance was constructed of granite that had been shipped from New York, with an interior and exterior set of large wooden doors that were bolted together with iron rivets. Incredibly, the original doors of the fort are still in use today.

In April 1833, Fort Pulaski was officially named in honor of Gen. Casimir Pulaski. Completed by 1847, this grand fortress had been built with 25 million bricks manufactured at the Hermitage Plantation just outside Savannah and stronger bricks from Alexandria, Virginia, and Baltimore, Maryland. Granite was shipped from New York, and sandstone came from Connecticut. The US government spent more than $1 million on the project. Although capable of holding 150 guns, in 1840, just 20 were mounted. Additional guns would be added by Confederate troops. Following its capture in 1862, Brig. Gen. Quincy Gillmore described Fort Pulaski as "a brick-work of five sides, or faces, including the gorge; casemated on all sides; walls seven and a half feet thick, and twenty-five feet high above high water; mounting one tier of guns in embrasures, and one en barbette. The gorge is covered by an earthen outwork (demilune) of bold relief." He added that the moat was seven to eight feet deep.

The Cockspur Island Lighthouse, built between 1837 and 1839, helped direct ships coming up the Savannah River prior to the Civil War. However, the structure was destroyed by a hurricane in 1854. The following year, John Norris, a New York architect, was contracted to rebuild and enhance the lighthouse to have a more permanent illuminating system. The lighthouse would contain five lamps with 14-inch reflectors that could signal up to nine miles. During the massive bombardment on April 10, 1862, the lighthouse stood helplessly between the lines of Confederate and Union cannon fire. Amazingly, the small brick beacon suffered only minor damage during the battle. The Cockspur Lighthouse is part of the Fort Pulaski National Monument Preserve. (FPNM.)

The Tybee Lighthouse, which stood near the oceanfront, served as a guard station and lookout during the war by both Confederate and Union soldiers. Confederate troops used it until November 1861, when they received word that the Union army had captured Port Royal, Beaufort, and Hilton Head, South Carolina. Upon their evacuation, the Confederates set fire to the lighthouse, destroying the wood interior. When the Union troops arrived on Tybee Island, they repaired the lighthouse and used it to observe activity at Fort Pulaski and direct the construction of their gun emplacements for the upcoming bombardment. (FPNM.)

# *Three*

# WAR DIVIDES THE NATION

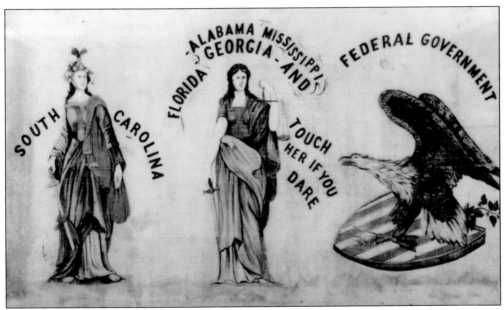

This original flag of Georgia secession was paraded through the streets of Savannah on the night of December 26, 1860. The banner represented growing support of South Carolina's decision to secede from the United States. The phrase "TOUCH HER IF YOU DARE" was meant to warn the United States that if it tried to force South Carolina back into the Union, Alabama, Florida, Mississippi, and Georgia would come to her aid. After intense debates among the state legislators in the capital city of Milledgeville, the state followed South Carolina, with its delegates voting 208-89 to adopt an ordinance of secession on January 19, 1861. The union of the United States was beginning to disintegrate. This magnificent artifact of the period is on exhibit in the Fort Pulaski Visitor Center. (FPNM.)

Abraham Lincoln (1809–1865) and Jefferson Davis (1808–1889) were presented with the responsibility of preserving and defending their respective nations. The fortifications, which had been built to protect the United States, would become battlefields and produce a new age of warfare that would ultimately be the downfall of these mighty fortresses. On April 29, 1861, President Davis sent a message to the Congress of the Confederate States of America, addressing President Lincoln's refusal to negotiate the issues of government properties with the Confederacy and the consequent dilemma that led to the firing on Fort Sumter. Davis addressed Lincoln and the world, stating, "All we want is to be let alone." (LOC.)

Georgia governor Joseph Emerson Brown (1821–1894) awaited the government's response to the secession of South Carolina. Born a South Carolinian, he was raised in northern Georgia. When tensions escalated between the North and South, Brown took measures to prepare Georgia militarily by acquiring federal military equipment and seeking out contractors to produce war materials to defend the state. He would later give perhaps the most significant orders of his administration: seize Fort Pulaski in the name of the state of Georgia. (Georgia State Archives.)

Gen. Alexander R. Lawton (1818–1896) first became a colonel of the 1st Georgia Regulars when Americans began choosing sides. On January 3, 1861, he ordered the seizure of Fort Pulaski. He attained the rank of brigadier general in April 1861 and was transferred to Virginia, serving as commander of Lawton's Brigade in the Army of Northern Virginia. During the Battle of Sharpsburg (Antietam), Maryland, he was wounded. Following his recovery, Lawton was appointed quartermaster general of the Confederacy. Due to his popularity and achievements, an earthwork fort built along the Savannah River and a prison constructed in Millen, Georgia, were named in his honor. (FPNM.)

The Republican Blues, a prominent militia unit raised in Savannah, had a long military career prior to the war, and continued its service in the Confederate army from 1861 to 1865. The unit was featured on the front cover of *Harper's Weekly* when the soldiers visited New York City prior to the separation between North and South. This sketch exhibits the fine uniforms the soldiers wore just prior to the war. Shortly after the seizure of Fort Pulaski, the men were issued uniforms and equipment more suited for the rigors of combat. (FPNM.)

Formed in 1842, the Irish Jasper Greens, named after Sgt. William Jasper and made up primarily of Irish immigrants, were among the first Confederate troops to capture Fort Jackson, Fort Pulaski, and the other forts protecting Savannah. The troops garrisoned Fort Pulaski and Fort Jackson in the early years of the war, but they were transferred to defend Atlanta in the summer of 1864. This elaborate monument towers over the graves of 28 members of the Irish Jasper Greens and prominent Catholic priest Peter Whelan in Savannah's Catholic Cemetery.

Maj. Gen. Lafayette McLaws (1821–1897), a graduate of West Point Military Academy, remained loyal to Georgia when the war began. First assigned to Fort Pulaski and other defenses of Savannah, he was soon transferred to Virginia, serving as a division commander under Gen. James Longstreet in the 1st Corps of the Army of Northern Virginia. Although they had been boyhood friends, Longstreet relieved McLaws of command in 1863 over disagreements in military strategies. McLaws was reassigned to Savannah only to endure the siege of the city in December 1864. He helped supervise the evacuation of Confederate forces into South Carolina, where they moved on to North Carolina to serve under Gen. Joseph Johnston in the final battles of the war. McLaws returned to Savannah and was later buried in Laurel Grove Cemetery. (LOC.)

In 1861, Savannah native Gilbert Moxley Sorrel was serving as a clerk with the Central Georgia Railroad. However, when his militia unit, the Georgia Hussars, was called to serve in the new Confederate army, he rushed to the opportunity, assisting in the seizure of Fort Pulaski. His unit was later transferred to the defenses on Skidaway Island. Sorrel was eager to "see the elephant," so he offered his military services and administrative skills to Gen. James Longstreet, serving as his aide-de-camp throughout the war. He finished the war as a general and returned home to continue his private life as a successful businessman. Sorrel is buried in the family mausoleum in Savannah's Laurel Grove Cemetery. (LOC.)

Although Georgia had not made its official decision to join South Carolina and other Southern states in seceding from the Union, on January 3, 1861, Georgia state troops left downtown Savannah on the steamship Ida, landing at the dock of Fort Pulaski by midday. With only a caretaker and a sergeant of the US Army on the premises, the fort was surrendered without any shots being fired. (FPNM.)

The Confederate soldiers quickly ran to the parapets, lowering the US flag and raising the Georgia secession flag. The flag has been noted in historical accounts to have been a banner with a white field and a single red star in the center. During the 150th anniversary of the seizure of Fort Pulaski, Confederate living historians recreated the scene of January 3, 1861. (Both photographs by Joel Cadoff, FPNM.)

Col. Charles Hart Olmstead (1837–1926) became an officer of the 1st Georgia Regulars, CSA, and was assigned to defend Fort Pulaski with just 385 soldiers. After a severe bombardment, he made the difficult decision of surrendering his sword to Maj. Charles G. Halpine. Colonel Olmstead and his men were later released from prison and returned to active duty in the Confederate army. He later served in the Atlanta Campaigns and was wounded on July 21, 1864, in the fighting around Decatur. Olmstead was with the Army of Tennessee when it was surrendered on April 26, 1865, at Bennett Place, near Durham Station, North Carolina. He returned to his native Savannah, where he was later buried in Laurel Grove Cemetery. (FPNM.)

On Thursday, December 26, 1861, Maj. Charles H. Olmstead was elected by the garrison to serve as post commander of Fort Pulaski. He later wrote, "With the dawn the air was filled with the sound of martial music and by 8 o'clock the commands that had been designated for the service were down at the wharf ready to embark on the little steamer . . . the balconies of the various stores and counting rooms overlooking the water were filled with people waving their handkerchiefs and cheering." (FPNM.)

Colonel Olmstead reflected on the pride he and his men felt when taking Fort Pulaski. "I can shut my eyes now and see it all now, the proud step of officers and men, the colors snapping in the strong breeze from the ocean, the bright sunlight of the parade as we emerged from the shadow of the archway, the first glimpse of a gun through an open casemate door. One and all they were photographed on my mind and will never be forgotten." (Photograph by Joel Cadoff, FPNM.)

The newly formed Confederate States of America quickly raised its national colors over Fort Pulaski and all other fortifications and government buildings across their country. This detailed sketch in *Harper's Weekly* depicts Confederate soldiers outside the fort on parade with their proud banner flying over their newly acquired fort. (LOC.)

Originally known as the first national flag of the Confederate States of America, this flag became more fondly known as the Stars & Bars. It replaced the initial secession flag that flew over Fort Pulaski earlier in the capture. However, the Confederate flag would only fly over the fort for about a year before Union troops retook the fort in April 1862.

Five companies made up the Confederate garrison of Fort Pulaski. Company B, Oglethorpe Light Infantry, under Capt. Thomas W. Sims; the German Volunteers, commanded by Capt. John H. Stegin; the Washington Volunteers, under Capt. John McMahon; the Irish Jasper Greens, commanded by Capt. John Foley; and the Montgomery Guards. They were all members of the 1st Regiment of Georgia Volunteers who defended the fort. The Macon Wise Guards, a company of the 25th Georgia Regulars, joined as part of the garrison. The total strength was 385 officers and men. Col. Charles H. Olmstead of the 1st Georgia Volunteer Regiment was in command. The fort was reinforced with 48 guns of different caliber and range. Although primarily infantrymen when they seized Fort Pulaski, the soldiers quickly began learning artillery drill to withstand the more serious threats yet to come.

Father Peter Whelan (1802–1871), an Irish immigrant, served as chaplain for the Montgomery Guards and was with the garrison at Fort Pulaski during the bombardment. Following the capture, Whelan was imprisoned with fellow soldiers at Governor's Island in New York Harbor, but was eventually paroled and returned to Savannah. In June 1864, he traveled to Andersonville Prison to tend to the soldiers, but contracted disease and returned to Savannah. Whelan died in February 1871 and was given a grand funeral before being laid to rest in Catholic Cemetery. One Confederate veteran stated, "I followed this good old man to his grave with a sense of exultation as I thought of the welcome that awaited him from the Master whose spirit he had caught and made the rule of his life." (FPNM.)

On the ramparts facing Tybee Island were five 8-inch and four 10-inch Columbiad cannon, one 24-pounder Blakely rifled cannon, and two 10-inch seacoast mortars. In the casemates bearing on Tybee were one 8-inch Columbiad and four 32-pounder guns, while in earthen batteries outside the fort were two 12-inch and one 10-inch seacoast mortars. The remaining guns were mounted to command the North Channel of the Savannah River and the marsh waterways to the southwest. (FPNM.)

Commodore Josiah Tattnall, who was placed in charge of the Savannah River defenses, traveled around the city with William Russell, a correspondent of the London *Times*, to show him the strong fortifications guarding Savannah. The Confederacy worked tirelessly on a public relations campaign throughout the war to gain the support of other nations in their war for independence. (LOC.)

Fort James Jackson, originally part of the Second System of fortifications of the United States, now occupied by Confederate forces, had an armament consisting of two 8-inch Columbiads, two 32-pounder rifled guns, and three 32-pounder naval guns. Two 12-pounder mountain howitzers guarded the rear of the fort.

The Oglethorpe Barracks were constructed in the city of Savannah in the mid-1820s to support the US troops who rotated duties from Fort Jackson and Fort Pulaski. Soldiers trained and sharpened their skills in between garrison duties at the outer defenses of the city. Confederate troops continued to use these military quarters in a similar fashion throughout the war. (FPNM.)

*Four*

# THEY CANNOT BREACH YOUR WALLS

As the Southern defenders of Fort Pulaski prepared hastily for the Union bombardment, their elite commander assured them that the fortress was impregnable. In a letter to Colonel Olmstead, Gen. Robert E. Lee guaranteed the fort's commander they would prevail in any bombardment. Lee wrote, "Colonel, they will make it pretty warm for you here with shells, but they cannot breach your walls at that distance." Lee was unaware that the newly invented rifled cannon was about to dismantle the masonry masterpiece he had helped construct earlier in his military career. (FPNM.)

While stationed near Coosawhatchie, South Carolina, General Lee visited Fort Pulaski in November 1861. On February 23, 1862, he wrote his wife, Mary, describing the challenges of fortifying Charleston and Savannah. "His gunboats are pushing up all the creeks and marshes of Savannah, and have attained a position so near the river as to shell the steamers navigating it. None have as yet been struck. I am engaged in constructing a line of defense at Fort Jackson which, if time permits and guns can be obtained, I hope will keep them out. They can bring such overwhelming force in all their movements that it has the effect to demoralize our new troops." Although Fort Pulaski fell, the Confederates succeeded in maintaining their defenses until December 1864. (LOC.)

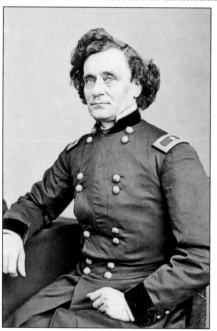

On October 29, 1862, Gen. Thomas W. Sherman led a Union force of 51 warships carrying 12,500 soldiers to capture Fort Walker and Fort Beauregard protecting Port Royal Sound and Beaufort, South Carolina. Following their capture, Sherman was given charge over the Department of the South until he was deemed ineffective by the federal government. Prior to the bombardment of Fort Pulaski, he was relieved of command by Gen. David Hunter. (FPNM.)

On November 7, 1861, at about 8:00 a.m., the Union fleet under the command of Capt. Samuel F. DuPont and led by the USS *Wabash* sailed into the Port Royal Sound and began a strategic bombardment against Forts Walker and Beauregard. Gen. Thomas Drayton, another West Point graduate, was in command of the overall defenses of Port Royal, but his small force of South Carolina and Georgia militia and regulars were no match for the Union force. After heavy exchanges of cannon fire between the forts and the ships for about four hours, the Confederates abandoned the forts, and the Union ships began landing infantry forces to complete the victory. (LOC.)

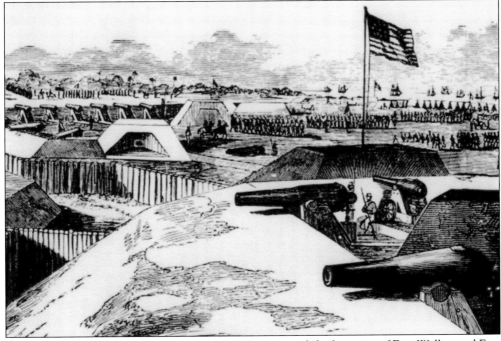

After some intense cannon fire between the US Navy and the batteries of Fort Walker and Fort Beauregard, the Confederate defenses along the southern South Carolina coast were taken, and the Union troops began to establish a foothold in order to begin their offensive into the Confederate mainland. Today, very little remains of these earthen fortifications. (LOC.)

Union forces began constructing quarters and warehouses around the Pope Plantation, which had been used as Confederate headquarters, while hauling in large quantities of military supplies to support their strategic operations to recapture federal property, including Fort Pulaski and Fort Sumter. This sketch shows Union works on Hilton Head. (LOC.)

Once Union forces established a secure base of operations along the coastal areas of the South, they began to plan the recapture of key masonry forts. In April 1862, Fort Macon in North Carolina would fall, along with Fort Pulaski in Georgia and Fort Clinch in Florida. Fort Sumter and Fort Moultrie in South Carolina remained in Confederate possession until the end of the war, but Charleston Harbor was essentially cut off from resupply for the remainder of the conflict. (LOC.)

As the Confederate outposts on the beaches of Tybee Island saw the approach of the Union fleet, the Southern soldiers withdrew toward the defenses of Fort Pulaski and other fortifications. In their retreat, they burned the Tybee Lighthouse. (LOC.)

As the threat of attack was felt by the Confederate defenders, General Lee instructed Colonel Olmsted to take precautionary measures for a potential bombardment and a long siege. Large timbers were loaded on barges and sailed to Fort Pulaski. They were then placed over the casemates, and dirt was built up along the base. Additional dirt was mounded up between the gun emplacements to protect the cannon. (FPNM.)

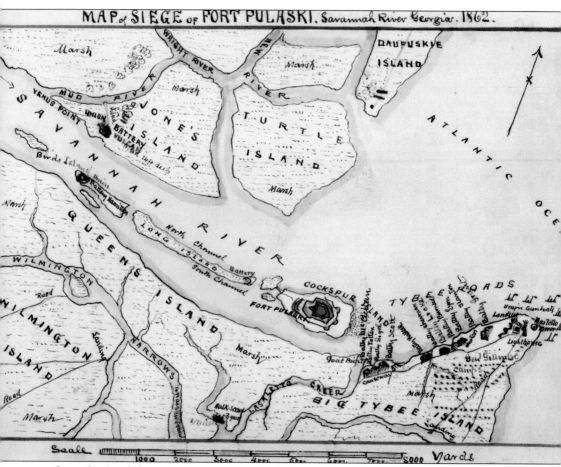

Once the Confederates had retreated to the defenses of Fort Pulaski and beyond, toward Savannah, Union forces moved in along the coastline and into the marshes and creeks to begin their siege of Fort Pulaski. (FPNM.)

## *Five*

# THE TEST OF STRENGTH

Maj. Gen. Quincy Adams Gillmore of Black River, Ohio, will always be remembered as the Union officer who initiated the first successful use of rifled cannon. Graduating first in his class of 1849 at West Point, Gillmore was first involved in the construction of fortifications to defend the United States, much like Robert E. Lee and others in their early military careers. When the Civil War erupted, Gillmore, then a captain, was sent to the Southern coast to help recapture the forts that had been seized by the Confederate armies. Until that time, smoothbore cannon were the only proven type of artillery. However, when the Union fleet landed on Georgia shores, Gillmore convinced Union headquarters that he could take Fort Pulaski by throwing a fierce bombardment at the fort with the new, untested, rifled cannon. (LOC.)

Whitelaw Reid, editor and publisher of the *New York Tribune*, described Gillmore in this manner: "Gillmore is a quick-speaking, quick-moving, soldierly man . . . a fine, wholesome looking, solid six footer, with big head, broad, good humored face, and a high forehead faintly elongated by a suspicion of baldness, curly brown hair and beard, and a frank open face." His greatest attribute as a soldier was a fearless disregard for tradition. At the Battle of Fort Pulaski, Gillmore was brevetted a brigadier general and later became a major general of volunteers. (LOC.)

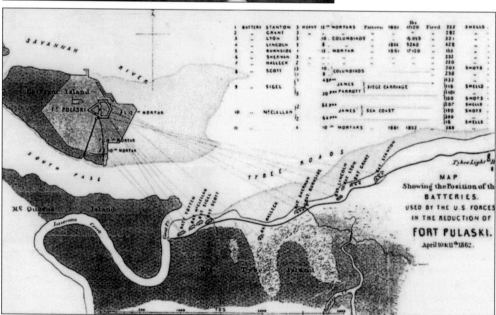

The Union command drew up the elaborate plans for the siege of Fort Pulaski. Gun batteries built of sand and logs would be constructed on Tybee Island and across the Savannah River on South Carolina's Jones, Turtle, and Daufuskie Islands. (FPNM.)

Col. Edward Wellman Serrell, 1st New York Engineers, was instrumental in guiding the construction of the batteries surrounding Fort Pulaski. He would later rise to the rank of general, serving as chief engineer for the Department of the South and the 10th Army Corps, followed by advancement to chief of staff of the Army of the James during the Richmond Campaigns in 1864. He served in more than 120 engagements during the Civil War. (LOC.)

The Union army began constructing wharfs and docks on Hilton Head Island to land and offload vast quantities of military supplies to commence their operations against Fort Pulaski and the defenses of Charleston. Hilton Head would become a military city and the base of operations for these coastal Union armies, numbering more than 30,000 troops during the war. (LOC.)

The 1st New York Engineers were heavily involved in the supervision and actual construction of the immense batteries, which had to be erected around Fort Pulaski to be any help in the success of the siege operations. Here, Company F of the 1st New York Engineers stands in formation at the additional barracks and quarters that had been built just beyond Fort Pulaski following the capture of the fort. (LOC.)

Union soldiers began the arduous work of building the siege positions out of sand and pine logs. Thomas Jones of the 48th New York wrote in a letter home, "When we came to Daufuskie Island they set us to work carrying pine logs on our shoulders about the distance from one and one half to two miles. There were 20,000 poles and we carried them in nine days." General Gilmore would later state in his official report that the regiments of the 48th New York and 7th Connecticut hauled 1,900 poles over a mile to the location of Jones Island, where a wharf was built to receive supplies. (FPNM.)

The 48th New York Infantry were sketched during their construction of Battery Vulcan on Jones Island, South Carolina. This series of sketches depicts guards on duty, the destruction of the communication lines for the Confederates, and the night work of building Battery Vulcan. (LOC.)

Battery Vulcan at Venus Point on Jones Island is depicted in this newspaper sketch illustrating the battery and Union troops ready for the siege of Fort Pulaski, visible in the distance. (LOC.)

The 1st New York Engineers were instrumental in building the siege works against both Fort Pulaski and Fort Wagner, South Carolina. This photograph shows the soldiers digging siege lines behind a rolling gabion in front of Fort Wagner. Similar methods were used in building the earthen batteries around Fort Pulaski, and in the initial stages, the men worked at night so they would not be detected by Confederate sentries. They camouflaged their work with brush and rested during the day. Eventually, when their defenses were tall enough and strong enough, they brought in artillery and ammunition to prepare for the bombardment. (LOC.)

Battery Lincoln was one of the 11 earthen and log batteries built by Union troops around Fort Pulaski. This battery position was on Tybee Island and served three 8-inch Model 1844 Columbiads, which were approximately two miles in range of the fort. In the 19-hour bombardment, the guns at Battery Lincoln fired 428 shells, about once every 2.66 minutes. (Sketch by W.T. Crane, FPNM.)

A total of 10 batteries and 36 guns were directed toward Fort Pulaski: Battery Stanton with three heavy 13-inch mortars set at 3,400 yards; Battery Grant with three heavy 13-inch mortars set at 3,200 yards; Battery Lyon with three heavy 10-inch Columbiads set at 3,100 yards; Battery Lincoln with three heavy 8-inch Columbiads at 3,045 yards; Battery Burnside with one heavy 13-inch mortar at 2,750 yards; Battery Sherman with three heavy 13-inch mortars at 2,650 yards; Battery Halleck with two heavy 13-inch mortars at 2,400 yards; Battery Scott with three 10-inch Columbiads and one 8-inch Columbiad at 1,670 yards; Battery Sigel with five 30-pounder Parrott rifled cannon, one 48-pounder James rifled cannon (former 24 pounders), and two 84-pounder James rifled cannon at 1,650 yards; and Battery McClellan with two 84-pounder James rifled cannon (former 42 pounders) and two 64-pounder James rifled cannon (former 32-pounders) at 1,650 yards. (LOC.)

Invented by Robert Parker Parrott in 1861, this 30-pounder Parrott rifled gun is similar to those used to bombard Fort Pulaski. It weighed 4,200 pounds and held a charge of 3.25 pounds of black powder with a projectile of 24–29 pounds. It had a range of 4,800 yards (2.7 miles) but a maximum range of 8,453 yards (4.8 miles). Lou Evans of the 48th New York State Volunteers, Company F, reactivated, stands by the gun on the southwest bastion of Fort Pulaski.

The James rifled cannon was recently developed by Charles T. James, a Rhode Island native who was self taught in mathematics and mechanics. The siege of Pulaski served as their testing ground, and they were an obvious success. However, these guns were retired soon thereafter, as continued advancements were made in the engineering of artillery. James continued to help develop new artillery technology, but during a demonstration of a new projectile at Sag Harbor, Long Island, New York, a worker attempted to remove a cap from a shell. It exploded, killing the man and mortally wounding James, who died the next day. (LOC.)

This unusual looking artillery shell known as the "James Shot" was developed by Charles T. James. It has a birdcage type of design at the base, which helped propel the shell farther and more accurately. The weight of each shell varied from 48 pounds to 64 pounds, depending on whether it was designated for the 48-pounder, the 64-pounder, or the 84-pounder gun. (FPNM.)

The first major shot of the Civil War came from a mortar being launched on Fort Sumter early in the morning of April 12, 1861, by Capt. George S. James, who ignited a 10-inch seacoast mortar. Shortly after the war began, the Union military developed the 13-inch siege mortar. These were mounted in place around the perimeter of Fort Pulaski. They carried a 227-pound shell fired from 20 pounds of gunpowder with a range of more than 4,000 yards. These could do serious damage. (LOC.)

Maj. Gen. David Hunter, a West Point graduate and veteran of the Battle of Bull Run, Virginia, had replaced Gen. Thomas W. Sherman as overall commander of the Department of the South. Once the batteries had been constructed and the adequate number of cannon placed in position, Hunter was ready to receive the surrender of Colonel Olmstead either peaceably or by force. (LOC.)

At 5:30 a.m. on April 10, 1862, Major General Hunter sent 1st Lt. James Wilson with a support staff by boat to the fort to demand its surrender. The surrender terms read, "I hereby demand of you the immediate surrender and restoration of Fort Pulaski to the authority and possession of the United States. This demand is made with a view of avoiding, if possible, the effusion of blood which must result from the bombardment and attack now in readiness to be opened. The number, caliber, and completeness of the batteries surrounding you leave no doubt as to what must result in case of your refusal; and as the defense, however obstinate, must eventually succumb to the assailing force at my disposal, it is hoped you may see fit to avert the useless waste of life." (LOC.)

Olmstead was given just 30 minutes to reply, and during that time he ordered his men to their posts. He then sent his reply to Lieutenant Wilson, who was waiting at the fort's wharf. In his reply, Olmstead stated, "I have to acknowledge receipt of your communication of this date demanding the unconditional surrender of Fort Pulaski. In reply I can only say that I am here to defend the fort, not to surrender it. I have the honor to be, very respectfully your obedient servant, Chas. H. Olmstead, Colonel, First Volunteer Regiment of Georgia, commanding Post." (FPNM.)

After General Hunter received his disagreeable response from Olmstead, he ordered all batteries to prepare for action. At about 8:15 a.m. on April 10, 1862, the order was given to open fire. The first shot came from Battery Halleck, which was a 13-inch mortar. A constant barrage of shells was thrown upon the fort throughout the day and into the evening. By 2:00 p.m., the southeastern walls had been breached. The hole was so wide that the arches of the casemate were laid bare. (FPNM.)

Union batteries continued the concentrated bombardment on Fort Pulaski throughout the day. This newspaper sketch depicts the firing of a mortar toward the fort. (LOC.)

Pvt. L.W. Landershine, a Confederate soldier of the 1st Georgia Volunteer Infantry who was inside the fort during the bombardment, described the battle in his account of April 10–11, 1862: "The sound of the balls and shells coming through the air at first had to my ear an unpleasant sound, but I soon got used to them and listened to them with pleasure. We gave different guns names from the peculiarity of their firing. One we styled "Rocket" this one we feared more than all the others. We no sooner saw the smoke than we could hear the ball whiz by the fort. By afternoon the port holes of the casemates in the South face of the fort had been greatly enlarged by the enemy and their shots and shells were coming into the casemates." (FPNM.)

When the cannonade began, the local newspaper made the announcement, sending the citizens of Savannah into fear and apprehension. L.T. Brome wrote, "April 10th, At six o'clock this morning, the Federals opened a heavy fire on Fort Pulaski. The explosion of the shells can be seen from the bay. Heavy firing in the direction of Fort Pulaski this morning. Shells plainly visible from the city. Five of the enemy's batteries commenced an attack on Fort Pulaski at six o'clock this morning. The fort replies slowly and deliberately. The enemy's shells appear to burst some distance over the Fort. No apprehensions are felt here in regard to the safety of the fort. The bombardment continues heavy." (LOC.)

During the intense bombardment, one of Olmstead's greatest concerns became the threat of the Union artillery shells getting closer to the gunpowder magazine on the northwest corner of the fort.

After 30 hours of ferocious destruction by Union artillery, Colonel Olmstead had his men raise the white flag of surrender over the battered fort. As the flag became visible to the Union soldiers in their batteries, a ceasefire was ordered, and the soldiers began to cheer with great excitement. More than 5,000 shells had been launched at Fort Pulaski during the bombardment. (FPNM.)

The officers of North and South gathered by candlelight in Colonel Olmstead's quarters, where the Confederates surrendered their swords to Maj. Charles G. Halpine, sent as a representative of General Hunter's command. The terms of surrender for the Confederate soldiers were unconditional. Later that evening, the Southern soldiers formed by companies on the parade ground, stacked their arms, and marched to quarters for the night. The US flag was raised once again over Fort Pulaski, this time permanently. (FPNM.)

Colonel Olmstead's sword is on exhibit in the visitor center at Fort Pulaski. Upon surrendering his sword to Major Halpine, Colonel Olmstead stated, "I yield my sword, but I trust I have not disgraced it." (FPNM.)

Gen. Charles Halpine, an Irish immigrant, was a correspondent for the *New York Times* prior to the war. He enlisted in the 69th New York Infantry Regiment, later joining General Hunter's staff, serving as assistant adjutant general. While stationed at Hilton Head, Halpine continued writing, contributing to the *New York Herald* under the pseudonym of "Miles O'Reilly." He wrote *Life and Adventures, Songs, Services, and Speeches of Private Miles O'Reilly, 47th Regiment New York Volunteers, 1864,* and *Baked Meats of the Funeral, a Collection of Essays, Poems, Speeches, and Banquets, by Private Miles O'Reilly, late of the 47th Regiment New York Volunteer Infantry.* Halpine ultimately became a brigadier general. However, he left the US Army in 1864 due to his weakening eyesight. In 1868, Halpine died from an accidental overdose of chloroform. (LOC.)

Gen. Hugh Weedon Mercer, a West Point graduate, chose to join the Confederate cause and was stationed in Savannah at the time of the collapse of Fort Pulaski. On April 14, 1862, Mercer wrote of the fall of the once impressive fort: "It is with a sad heart that I chronicle (I could not do it before) the unconditional surrender of Fort Pulaski. It fell about 2 o'clock on April 11th, after some thirty hours bombardment. This result has stunned and surprised us all. We felt that the fort was doomed but did not dream that it could be reduced in thirty hours!" (LOC.)

The once grand, invincible fortress, which took more than 15 years to build, took less than 30 hours to demolish and demoralize its defenders. Had the bombardment continued, Fort Pulaski would have been reduced to a pile of rubble like its neighboring fort in Charleston Harbor, Fort Sumter. In his report to Union army headquarters, Gen. Quincy Gilmore wrote, "This success so fully demonstrates the power and effectiveness of rifled cannon, for breaching at long distances, at distances indeed hitherto untried, and considered altogether impracticable, thus opening a new era in the use of this most valuable and comparatively unknown arm of service." (FPNM.)

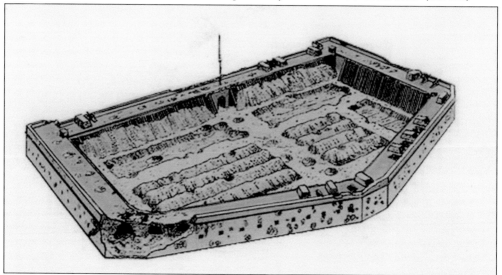

Prior to the siege, General Lee had advised the Confederate garrison to dig trenches throughout the parade ground to prevent artillery shells from rolling around and ricocheting inside the fort, which would have caused even further damage and destruction. This diagram shows the design work for the protection of the interior and the devastation on the southeast corner of the fort. (FPNM.)

This wartime photograph shows the earlier defensive work done by the Confederate troops prior to the bombardment. The wooden timbers mounted along the casemate entrances to protect the quarters and garrison helped the interior, but it was ultimately the exterior of the fort that withstood horrific damage. (FPNM.)

The top of the fort received much destruction during the cannonade, knocking out the Confederate guns. This wartime photograph taken after Union forces entered the fort reveals at least two guns and a mortar that had been put out of operation. (FPNM.)

The photograph above shows the same area of the fort, with Union soldiers posing to the left of the destroyed gun emplacement. Below, this splendid wartime sketch of the same subject is a detailed depiction of the destruction during the cannonade that knocked out the Confederate guns. (Both, FPNM.)

Another wartime photograph shows a mortar inside Fort Pulaski, completely destroyed during the bombardment. (FPNM.)

This gun appears to still be intact, but there is plenty of evidence of the destruction around it. As bricks began to chip and fly off the walls, it became more and more difficult for the Confederate soldiers to remain at their gun positions. Note in the left foreground a James shell (see page 56) resting on the ground of the parapet after sailing into the brick walls. (FPNM.)

This is another wartime photograph of a gun that also appears to still be serviceable, although the carriage and platform have deteriorated from the shot and shell. (FPNM.)

Union soldiers pose for a photograph inside one of the exposed casemates following the capture of the fort. This photograph clearly shows that the fort would have been completely demolished had the Confederates not capitulated as soon as they did. (FPNM.)

This Union soldier poses beside a flanking howitzer, which was located in the bastions. These guns were designed to defend the drawbridge from an infantry attack. However, they stood silent during the bombardment. (FPNM.)

This is a wider view of the parapet of Fort Pulaski following the bombardment. Broken bricks and piles of debris are evident. Note that the gun on the right was hit by a shell, breaking off the tip of the barrel. (FPNM.)

When the National Park Service began restoration efforts, they were able to locate some of the original guns from Fort Pulaski that had been engaged in the battle. This is the gun that had its barrel shot away.

This photograph taken in 2014 shows the barrel damage this gun sustained during the battle more than 150 years ago. Also note the brickwork damage left by the National Park Service to show the battle scars of the fort.

This wartime photograph is one of the rare images of the entire fort showing the armament on top. (FPNM.)

When the Union troops moved into Fort Pulaski, they grabbed one of the most coveted trophies—the Confederate garrison flag. In their enthusiasm, the men cut up the flag and took pieces with them as souvenirs. The description of these fragments reads, "Pieces of Confederate Flag that floated from staff of Fort Pulaski, Ga. which surrendered April 11th 1862. The flag was torn in pieces by the Union Soldiers." These fragments are in the archival collection at Fort Pulaski. (FPNM.)

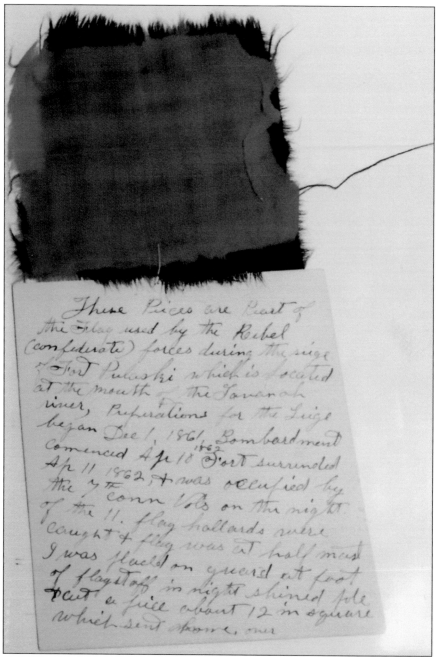

This is another significant piece of the history of Fort Pulaski that was donated to the National Park Service. James Gaye of the 7th Connecticut, the first regiment to garrison the fort, was on guard duty during the night and cut a piece of the Confederate flag for a keepsake of his participation in the battle. A segment of the card note card reads, "Preparations for the siege began December 1, 1861. Bombardment commence April 10, 1862. Fort surrendered April 11, 1862, and was occupied by the 7th Conn. Vols. On the night of the 11th. Flag hallards were caught & flag was at half mast. I was placed on guard at foot of flagstaff in night shined pole and cut a piece about 12 in. square which sent above." (FPNM.)

# Six

# UNDER THE STARS & STRIPES ONCE AGAIN

Pvt. William B. Howard, a soldier in the 48th New York State Volunteers, Company F, noted after the surrender of the fort that the US flag was flying over the fort once again. "April 12, 1862, This morning the Stars & strips [sic] are waving from the ramparts for Pulaski. The fleet runs up the river to the Fort." (New York State Military Museum and Veterans Research Center.)

During the bombardment, the 7th Connecticut Volunteer Infantry Regiment manned Batteries Totten, Halleck, Sherman, Lincoln, and Stanton. Following the capture, they would be the first Union troops to garrison Fort Pulaski. Colonel Terry was soon promoted to brigadier general and his second in command, Lt. Col. Joseph Hawley, took charge of the regiment. Terry went on to become commander of the 10th Army Corps and served in the US Army following the war. (LOC.)

Lt. Col. Joseph Hawley took charge of the 7th Connecticut Volunteer Infantry Regiment as colonel when Colonel Terry was promoted to general and transferred to Union headquarters on Hilton Head to help make preparations for the operations against Charleston. The 7th Connecticut was soon transferred to Hilton Head to engage on Morris Island, while the 48th New York Volunteer Regiment moved into the casemates and remained in garrison for more than a year. (LOC.)

The 48th New York State Volunteer Infantry, which was part of the siege operations of Fort Pulaski, moved into the fort and remained from mid-1862 to 1863. Mostly from Brooklyn, New York, the men distinguished themselves serving in the campaigns of the Battle of Fort Wagner on July 18, 1863, where they suffered the highest number of casualties among all white regiments engaged. The Battles of Olustee, Florida; Bermuda Hundred; Cold Harbor; Drewry's Bluff; and Petersburg, Virginia, were among their other honors. Their illustrious military career culminated in 1865 with the capture of Fort Fisher in North Carolina. (FPNM.)

This impressive view of the 48th New York on parade shows them extended across the field of Fort Pulaski. At the outset of the war, many units looked this sharp, but as the war intensified, casualties took severe tolls on appearances. By the end of the war, the 48th New York had lost 14 officers and 160 enlisted men killed in combat, 4 officers and 65 enlisted men as a result of wounds, and 2 officers and 121 enlisted men due to disease and other causes. A total of 20 officers and 346 enlisted men from this unit died during the war, of whom 1 officer and 53 enlisted men died as prisoners of war. (FPNM.)

Col. James H. Perry served as the first colonel of the 48th New York State Volunteers. A graduate of West Point and veteran of the Mexican-American War, he was a minister of the Methodist Church at the outbreak of the war. Perry rushed to the call to preserve the Union, raising a regiment in Brooklyn. The regiment would first become known as the Continental Guards until they were designated officially. During their early campaigns, they became known as "Perry's Saints," in honor of their beloved commander who died shortly after the regiment entered the gates of Fort Pulaski. (LOC.)

Soon after the regiment moved into Fort Pulaski, Colonel Perry died of apoplexy. Pvt. Thomas Jones, Company D, penned a letter to his sister Maggie E. Jones on June 20, 1862, detailing the loss of their respected colonel. He wrote, "We have lost our best friend and Colonel, James H. Perry. Yesterday, the 19th, he departed this life. He was in our quarter only the day before he died. He ate a hardy dinner and then he dropped off so suddenly." Jones continued writing, "We all feel it is a very heavy loss. I don't know what we will do now. We will never replace him." This image of Colonel Perry was printed on sheet music that the regimental band played during his funeral service at Fort Pulaski. Perry's body was later reinterred in Cypress Hills Cemetery in Brooklyn.

Colonel Perry was initially buried outside the fort's walls until his body could be transported home to Brooklyn. His gravestone reads, "A Noble Man. A Gallant Soldier. A Beloved Pastor. He Resigned His Pulpit To Die For His Country."

Following the unexpected death of Colonel Perry, the command was given to Lt. Col. William B. Barton, previously second in command of the regiment. He too was a graduate of West Point and continued to instill strict discipline in the ranks. Colonel Barton would prove to be a capable officer, ultimately leading a unit known as Barton's Brigade throughout much of the regiment's illustrious military career. (FPNM.)

Baseball had already become popular prior to the war. Here, behind a formation of a company of the 48th New York, soldiers are playing baseball. This is one of the first known, if not the very first, wartime photograph of soldiers playing baseball. Abraham J. Palmer, who wrote the history of the 48th New York State Volunteers, stated in his unit's history, "Our baseball nine was a fine success . . . it generally won the laurels. In a game with the 47th New York, played at Fort Pulaski, January 3, 1863, it won 20-7." (FPNM.)

As Fort Pulaski continued to be rebuilt by Union troops, it was never threatened again by Confederate forces. The officers and men began inviting their families to visit the fort by way of Union headquarters on Hilton Head. Henry P. Moore, a traveling photographer, took this unique wartime photograph of Colonel Barton and his wife with fellow officers of the 48th New York. Left of the Bartons stands Captain Elmendorf and Captain Elfwing and his dog. To the right of Mrs. Barton are Captain Eaton, 1st New York Engineers, who is leaning on the cascabel (knob) of the cannon; Captain Hurst; and Lieutenant Nichols. (FPNM.)

In November 1862, the wives and family of the officers visited Fort Pulaski for one of the grandest Thanksgiving Day celebrations remembered by the regiment. Games, dancing, music, theatrics by the Barton's Dramatics Association, and much eating took place inside the fort. (FPNM.)

The 48th New York had a fine regimental band. This is one of the best photographs of a wartime band assembled together. The regiment would lose drummer William Smith in the Battle of Cold Harbor in June 1864, in addition to others. (FPNM.)

While soldiers were garrisoned inside the fort, boredom set in frequently if they were not on duty. Some used their creativity to leave their lasting mark on the fort to let others know they had been there. These paintings are believed to have been done by members of the 48th New York regimental band. The one pictured here reads "H.Q. Drum Corps." (FPNM.)

More graffiti on the whitewashed walls reads, "The Union Now And Forever" with some type of star-like symbol underneath. Over the years, the graffiti fades out of existence. The author has noted the continuing deterioration over 25 years of visiting the fort. (FPNM.)

This third piece of graffiti is amusing, with the phrase "This Way Out" accompanying an artillery shell flying over the wall of the fort. (FPNM.)

Men of the 48th New York pose on top of the fort. From left to right are 1st Sgt. G. Morton, later second lieutenant, wounded at Fort Wagner; 1st Lt. J. Taylor, later wounded in the Battle of Fort Wagner, Battle of Olustee, Battle of Drewry's Bluff, and Battle of Cold Harbor; Capt. W.B. Coan, who would later become the third colonel of the regiment and was wounded at the Battle of Fort Wagner, Battle of Olustee, and Battle of Fort Fisher; and Adj. Christopher Hale, wounded at the Battle of Fort Wagner and discharged due to disability on October 19, 1864. (FPNM.)

Traces of the soldiers who lived within these walls are still evident with graffiti such as this inscription by John Charters, who was 19 years old when he enlisted as a private in the 48th New York Volunteers in August 1861. Charters endured many battles after leaving Fort Pulaski in 1863. When he mustered out of Company C in September 1865, he had earned the rank of sergeant. (FPNM.)

Regiments obtained a variety of pets throughout the war to improve morale among the men. The 48th New York documents having had a goat as a mascot until it mysteriously disappeared later in its career. This photograph of a dog and a soldier at Fort Pulaski shows another mascot of the regiment.

As the fort continued to be rebuilt, artillery drill was an important part of the soldiers' daily routine in continuing to defend their foothold on the Georgia coast. The 3rd Rhode Island Heavy Artillery joined the 48th New York at Fort Pulaski and helped train the infantry soldiers in the use of artillery. Together, these units trained on the cannon and would later cooperate on expeditions through the coastal interior, disrupting Confederate operations. Here, the 3rd Rhode Island Heavy Artillery demonstrates the procedures of loading and firing. Note that the timbers and dirt over the casemates have been removed, and the parade ground has been filled from the damage of the bombardment. This photograph was taken in 1863. (FPNM.)

This is another superb wartime photograph of the 3rd Rhode Island Artillery carrying on with artillery drill. Note what appears to be a "hot shot" furnace below. This no longer exists inside the fort. (FPNM.)

This gun crew of the 3rd Rhode Island poses in a gun emplacement for a close-up photograph. The gun they man was named "Burnside" after Gen. Ambrose Burnside, a fellow Rhode Islander. (FPNM.)

Outside the front gates of the fort, a city of buildings was constructed to provide housing for additional troops, supplies, ammunition, hospitals, kitchens, livestock, and sutlers. Here, officers of the 48th New York pose for the photograph. From left to right are Capt. James Farrell, Capt. A. Elmendorf, and Lieutenant V.R.K. Hilliard. (FPNM.)

This photograph of the southwest bastion reveals the massive operations just outside the fort's walls. Tons of ammunition, weapons, food, and other supplies were shipped in from the Union headquarters and supply base on Hilton Head. These soldiers of the 48th New York relax by the gun named "Sprague." (FPNM.)

The officers of the 48th New York State Volunteer Regiment stand together in this photograph at Fort Pulaski. The regiment's original commanding officer, Col. James H. Perry, had already died when this photograph was taken. Perry's Saints would lose 18 more officers in combat during the war, making it one of the 10 regiments with the highest number of officers killed in action. (FPNM.)

This lone Union sentry stands a vigilant watch on top of the peaceful walls of Fort Pulaski. Note there are still signs of the damage from the bombardment. (FPNM.)

A Union sentry stands guard at the northwest corner on top of the fort. The village of warehouses, ammunition storage, and hospitals are in the distance at the wharf. Signs of damage from the bombardment still remain. (FPNM.)

One of the outermost defensive positions for the Confederate soldiers was a Martello tower, which had been constructed on Tybee Island just after the War of 1812. At the outset of the war, Confederate troops captured and armed the fortification with two 32-pounder cannon until Union forces drove them off Tybee. In this wartime photograph, a company of the 48th New York Volunteer Infantry stands guard duty in front of this unique fortification. Following the war, the tower and the defenses around it fell into ruin and were eventually torn down. (FPNM.)

Although Matthew Brady has been given much of the credit for the photographs of the Civil War, other superb photographers, including Timothy O'Sullivan (pictured), were on the battlefields taking captivating images. Born in Ireland in 1840, O'Sullivan came to New York with his parents at the age of two. As a teenager, he got a job as an apprentice to Brady. In 1861, O'Sullivan traveled with the Union armies to the Southern coasts in the midst of some horrific artillery firefights. Following the fall of Fort Pulaski, he documented the devastation. Timothy O'Sullivan died of tuberculosis at the young age of 42 on January 14, 1882. (LOC.)

While January 1, 1863, marks the date the Emancipation Proclamation issued by President Lincoln took effect, nearly nine months prior, following the fall of Fort Pulaski, Maj. Gen. David Hunter issued General Order No. 7 on April 13, 1862. It stated, "All persons of color lately held to involuntary service by enemies of the United States in Fort Pulaski and on Cockspur Island, Georgia, are hereby confiscated and declared free in conformity with law." This photograph shows freed African Americans on Tybee Island. (FPNM.)

# *Seven*

# IMPRISONMENT OF
# THE IMMORTAL 600

On October 23, 1864, Fort Pulaski became a prison for captured Confederate soldiers on the battlefronts. The majority of these men were Confederate officers, some 520, who had been held previously on Hilton Head, where they were used as human shields by the Union armies trying to capture Charleston. This was in retaliation for the Confederates defending Charleston Harbor who first used 50 Union officers in the same fashion. During their imprisonment, the Southern soldiers were given meager rations consisting of moldy bread, soured pickles, and limited water, which contributed to the many cases of starvation, dehydration, dysentery, and scurvy. Within the walls of Fort Pulaski, 13 Confederate soldiers died and were buried outside. The remaining men were transferred by ships back to the prison at Fort Delaware in March 1865.

Fort Delaware, a Second System fortification like Fort Pulaski, became used as a prison for captured Confederate soldiers, primarily officers. The fort received its infamous claim as a prison for what would become known as the Immortal 600, some 520 Confederate officers who would later be used along the Southern coast as shields against Confederate artillery firing on Union positions. (LOC.)

The *Crescent City*, a Union warship, began transporting the prisoners from Fort Delaware to Morris Island, South Carolina, on August 20, 1864. It was intensely hot for the prisoners crammed into the hull of the ship. One Confederate officer, Lt. George Finley, 56th Virginia Infantry, described the journey. The men were in "total darkness, without any clothing and drenched with perspiration." He added that the prisoners were given "few crackers with a bit of salt beef or bacon." When they arrived near Union headquarters at Hilton Head, they remained on the ship until the prison stockade on Morris Island was completed. (LOC.)

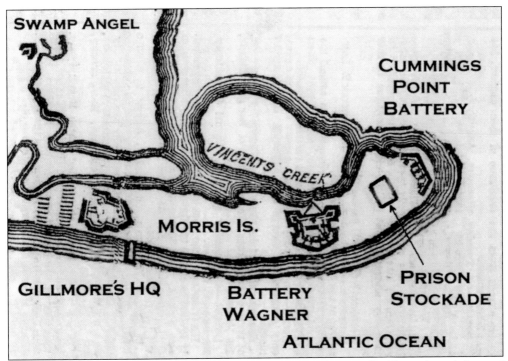

In retaliation for the Confederates using Union soldiers as human shields in their defense of Charleston Harbor, the Union forces used the same strategy by bringing captured Confederate officers to Morris Island and corralling them in a makeshift stockade. (LOC.)

This is a wartime photograph of the wooden stockade constructed along the beachfront of Morris Island, where Union forces held their defenses. In late August 1864, the 520 Confederate officers arrived by ship from Fort Delaware, Maryland. Soldiers of the 54th Massachusetts stood guard over the prisoners. After 45 days of exposure to the coastal sun, meager rations, and artillery fire between Confederate and Union forces, the prisoners were transferred to Fort Pulaski. Three Confederate officers died while imprisoned on Morris Island. (LOC.)

Col. Philip P. Brown, 157th New York State Volunteers, became the commandant of the prison at Fort Pulaski. His regiment was engaged in the Battles of Chancellorsville and Gettysburg, and was later transferred to South Carolina. The regiment eventually occupied Fort Pulaski. Brown tried to make the conditions tolerable for the Confederate prisoners, but on December 15, 1864, he was ordered to limit rations to only a quarter pound of bread, 10 ounces of cornmeal, and a half pint of pickles per day. One ounce of salt was issued to each prisoner every five days. The Confederate officers were forced to scavenge, which included rats, cats, dogs, and any other creature within arm's reach of the cells. When Savannah fell to Sherman's army, regular rations were issued. The prisoners were ultimately transferred back to Fort Delaware, and the 157th New York was mustered out on June 8, 1865. (United States Army Heritage and Education Center.)

This unique wartime photograph of the interior of Fort Pulaski reveals howitzers stretched along the quarters of the Union soldiers, facing the prison cells across the parade ground. It is highly likely that this photograph was taken during the imprisonment of the Immortal 600. (FPNM.)

Barred cells were installed inside the fort's casemates. Bunk beds were added, but no straw was provided to cushion the wooden slats. Life was cramped and miserable with little food and water. Capt. Henry Dickinson, 2nd Virginia Cavalry, held captive at Fort Pulaski, described their rations: "Our new ration of corn meal (sour), pickles, and seventy-five loaves of bread went into effect yesterday, and a terrible diet it is. That it will kill some is evident." (FPNM.)

Captain Dickinson provided additional descriptions of the misery. He described the death of Lt. George B. Fitzgerald, 12th Virginia Cavalry, Company A: "Two days ago, Lt. George B. Fitzgerald was taken to the hospital, and this morning announcement was made that 'Fitz is dead.' He was a confirmed opium eater; a poor, miserable wreck—ragged, filthy, lousy . . . He has had no blanket, no socks, hardly clothes to cover him; none of us could supply him, and he slept alone, covering himself with an old piece of tent fly . . . A graduate of West Point; a lieutenant in the old army, mingling with the Lees, McClellans and Grants." Fitzgerald was among the 13 Confederate officers buried outside the walls of Fort Pulaski. (FPNM.)

Capt. James Daniel Meadows (1827–1900) enlisted in Company A, 1st Alabama Infantry, CSA. He was captured on July 9, 1863, at Port Hudson, Louisiana. Meadows was sent to Fort Columbus (Fort Jay), New York, and then to Johnson's Island, Ohio. While there, he stated in a letter that he was shot in both legs while adjusting his coat by the privy. Meadows was later transferred to Point Lookout, Maryland, and then to Fort Delaware. He endured imprisonment at Morris Island and Fort Pulaski and the return to Fort Delaware. Meadows took the Oath of Allegiance on June 12, 1865, and returned home to his wife, Mary Jane Johnston Meadows. (Alabama State Archives.)

Lt. Thomas Stewart Armistead of Milton, Florida, enlisted in Company E, 8th Florida Infantry, in March 1862. Stewart was wounded twice, once in the knee at the Battle of Chancellorsville, Virginia, and then in the Battle of the Wilderness, where he was captured. After being imprisoned in northern camps, he was transferred to Morris Island and then to Fort Pulaski. Armistead was one of the fortunate, returning home to go into the ministry. He rests in Wildwood Cemetery in Bartow, Florida. (Pamela Lyons Hobbs.)

Capt. Thomas Fern Perkins was one of the more fascinating men of the Immortal 600. He enlisted in the Confederate army in June 1861, helping form a company of artillery. His unit was captured at the Battle of Fort Donelson, but Perkins managed to escape and return home to enlist in a cavalry unit. He joined Gen. Nathan Bedford Forrest's cavalry command and later rode with General Wheeler. Perkins was captured again in December 1863, near Franklin, Tennessee, and managed to escape temporarily, but was recaptured. Perkins was sent to the prison in Camp Chase and then on to Fort Delaware, where he became a member of the Immortal 600. He spent much time in solitary confinement but survived the war. Perkins made some 13 escape attempts from various prisons. (Williamson County Archives of Franklin, Tennessee.)

William James enlisted in the 55th Tennessee Infantry at Sumner County, Tennessee, in December 1861. He was promoted to captain of Company C, 44th Tennessee Infantry. James survived fighting in the battles of Shiloh, Tennessee; Perryville, Kentucky; Murfreesboro, Tennessee; and then the 1864 campaigns in Virginia of Bermuda Hundred, Chaffin's Farm, Weldon Railroad, and Drewry's Bluff. He made it through almost the entire war unscathed until he was captured at Petersburg, Virginia, on June 17, 1864. He was sent to Fort Delaware as a prisoner of war and then transferred to Morris Island. He went on to Fort Pulaski and finally returned to Fort Delaware. When the war drew to a close, James was released from Fort Delaware on April 18, 1865. (Michael E. James.)

Capt. Nero Guy Bedford, born March 16, 1825, enlisted in Company I of the 26th North Carolina Infantry. He became a prisoner of war and survived to go on and live a long life, dying on September 22, 1889. He was buried in Lone Oak Cemetery, Lake County, Florida.

Of the 520 Confederate soldiers, 13 died from the poor conditions suffered within the prison walls of Fort Pulaski. They were buried outside the fort in a mass grave. This is a contemporary painting by historical artist Martin Pate depicting the burial of the soldiers. (FPNM.)

In March 1865, the remaining prisoners were transported by ships back to the prison of Fort Delaware, where they remained until the end of the war. As a result of the filthy drinking water, meager rations, disease, and weather, 25 more of the Immortal 600 would die. By the end of the war, more than 30,000 Confederate soldiers and civilian prisoners had passed through the gates of Fort Delaware, and 2,500 soldiers had died. (LOC.)

The Confederate prisoners who perished at Fort Pulaski were finally memorialized on October 27, 2012. A monument is inscribed with their names: Lt. Iverson L. Burney, 49th Georgia Infantry, died November 12, 1864; Lt. George B. Fitzgerald, 12th Virginia Cavalry, Co. A, died November 13, 1864; Lt. Christopher C. Lane, 3rd North Carolina Infantry, died December 8, 1864; Lt. John M. Burgin, 22nd North Carolina Infantry, died January 28, 1865; Lt. Russell W. Legg, 50th Virginia Infantry, died February 7, 1865; Capt. Moses J. Bradford, 10th Missouri Infantry, died February 14, 1865; Capt. Alexander M. King, 50th Virginia Infantry, died February 16, 1865; Lt. Eli A. Rosenbalm, 37th Virginia Infantry, died February 17, 1865; Lt. Thomas J. Goodloe, 44th Tennessee Infantry, died February 27, 1865; Capt. O.R. Brumley, 20th North Carolina Infantry, died March 4, 1865; Lt. C. Byrd Eastham, 10th Virginia Infantry, died March 6, 1865; Lt. John T. Ganaway, 50th Virginia Infantry, died March 10, 1865; Capt. John H. Tolbert, 5th Florida Infantry, died March 14, 1865 (FPNM.)

The Confederate soldiers were memorialized on October 27, 2012, with a monument listing their names, recognizing those who perished inside Fort Pulaski. Here, Margie Blythe Poland gives remarks in memory of these noble Southern soldiers. (FPNM.)

For 150 years after these men perished in the prison of Fort Pulaski, their names were known only to God. Now they have long-lasting remembrance on earth. (FPNM.)

# *Eight*

# PRESERVATION OF A NATIONAL TREASURE

Maj. Gen. William Tecumseh Sherman and his staff devised the strategy of marching through the heart of Georgia and ultimately capturing the key port city of Savannah. Although the garrison of Fort Pulaski and surrounding Union posts had virtually closed this important city, arms, equipment, and food supplies were still being transferred by rail and wagons on the mainland to continue to support the Confederate cause. Pictured here are, from left to right, Gen. O.O. Howard, Gen. John A. Logan, Gen. William B. Hazen, Sherman, Gen. Jefferson C. Davis, Gen. Henry W. Slocum, and Gen. J.A. Mower. (LOC.)

General Sherman had led more than 60,000 Union soldiers from Atlanta to Savannah. However, the journey had originally begun as far north as Chattanooga, Tennessee. He would become one of the greatest generals in US history, but at the same time, one of the most despised of all Union generals for waging war against the Southern civilian population. (LOC.)

In December 1864, when Sherman's army approached the outskirts of Savannah, he detached Gen. William B. Hazen with over 5,000 troops of the XIV Corps to capture Fort McAllister in order to open the lines of communication between the Union navy and the Union army. The small garrison of just 200 Confederates could in no way withstand such an attack. In a matter of 15 minutes, Hazen's troops overran the fort. (LOC.)

Sgt. W.H. Andrews described in his memoirs that on "Tuesday night, December 20, 1864, the forces of Gen. Hardee evacuated the city of Savannah, Ga. The Regulars (1st Georgia Regulars) were withdrawn from the works about eleven o'clock, and I will never forget passing through the city which was sealed. Doors were being knocked down, guns firing in every direction, the bullets flying over and around us. Women and children screaming and rushing in every direction. All combined made it a night to never be forgotten by them who witnessed it. We finally reached the river where a string of rice barges strung end to end formed a bridge for us to cross on. The bridge was a poor makeshift, but the army succeeded in crossing it. While crossing the bridge, our way was lighted up by the burning of the Confederate gunboats (CSS *Georgia* and CSS *Savannah*) and other vessels lying in the Savannah River. Sad to look at, but at the same time made a beautiful picture on the water. After the army had crossed, the barges were cut loose and destroyed." (LOC.)

Gen. William Hardee had less than 10,000 combatants scattered over a massive front surrounding Savannah against Sherman's overwhelming force of 60,000 infantry and 5,000 cavalry. Ultimately, Hardee ordered the evacuation on the evening of December 20, 1864. Once in Hardeeville, South Carolina, the Confederate army marched north to escape Sherman's advance. (LOC.)

On December 22, 1864, General Sherman and his massive Union army rode into the streets of Savannah. He wrote in a telegram to Pres. Abraham Lincoln, "I beg to present you, as a Christmas gift, the city of Savannah, with 150 heavy guns and plenty of ammunition, and also about 25,000 bales of cotton." Between November 16 and December 10, the Union army had marched some 255 miles from Atlanta to Savannah. In January 1865, they would prepare for the final march through South Carolina and end the war in North Carolina. (LOC.)

On April 9, 1865, Gen. Robert E. Lee surrendered his exhausted and surrounded Southern army to Lt. Gen. Ulysses S. Grant in the small village of Appomattox Court House, Virginia. The war was now over in Virginia and would soon end across the country. (LOC.)

On April 26, 1865, Gen. Joseph Eggleston Johnston surrendered 89,270 Confederate soldiers to Maj. Gen. William Tecumseh Sherman at the farm of James and Nancy Bennett, near Durham Station, North Carolina. It was the largest surrender of the entire war. (Bennett Place State Historic Site.)

As the war drew to a close and soldiers returned home, there was still the duty of the US military to remain until the 14th and 15th Amendments were passed, law and order restored, and a devastated South assisted with rebuilding. Regiments including the 147th Illinois Infantry and 103rd USCT garrisoned Fort Pulaski and stood guard over some political prisoners through 1866. Here, Gene Smallwood, member of the 48th New York State Volunteers, reactivated, stands guard at the sally port.

Following the war, many of the forts, which had become military prisons midway through the conflict, were now confinement for incarcerated politicians who were primarily responsible for igniting the war. Some of the prisoners included Confederates James A. Seddon, secretary of war (pictured); George Trenholm, secretary of treasury; R.M.T. Hunter, secretary of the state; and the governors of South Carolina, Florida, and Alabama. (LOC.)

The 68th New York Infantry Regiment, which had fought in the Battles of Chancellorsville, Gettysburg, and the battles for Chattanooga, was ordered to coastal Georgia at the end of the war to serve as part of the Union occupation forces in the district of Savannah from July 1865 until November 1865. Col. Felix Prince Salm, commander of the regiment, was honorably discharged and mustered out his regiment on November 30, 1865, at Fort Pulaski. (LOC.)

Following the conclusion of the Civil War and the withdrawal of Union soldiers occupying the Southern states, military posts, including Fort Pulaski, were dramatically downsized in military personnel and in some cases closed. Rifled cannon had proven these masonry forts now obsolete to any attacker, and the US government was financially bankrupt and unable to sustain a large military force. Nevertheless, in order to keep Fort Pulaski viable, some enhancements were made to the demilune with underground powder magazines and gun emplacements just outside the fort from 1869 to 1872. More improvement plans had been made by the US Army Corps of Engineers, but they did not follow through due to the cost involved and the lack of any immediate threat.

By 1872, Fort Pulaski was closed as a military post. It was not until 1898 that the fort would once again experience military activity with the installation of more modern armament of that period and a new design of fortifications.

In April 1898, the United States prepared for war with Spain. Although many of the brick forts had been downsized and some closed, this unexpected threat of war was felt in the southern United States, and improvements in defense needed to be made. An innovative style of concrete bunkers had been incorporated into the Fort Pulaski defenses as well as other outdated brick forts. A battery was installed on the demilune of the fort and an iron carriage with an 8-inch breech loading gun was mounted. These guns provided additional defense to the mouth of the Savannah River. More walls and guns were implemented, including a minefield placed in the river just beyond the fort. (FPNM.)

To defend the mouth of the Savannah River, Battery Hambright was constructed on June 1, 1899. It was built with concrete and a metal framework and was named in honor of Horace George Hambright, an officer who died in 1896 while serving in the North Dakota Territory. The battery had an armament of two 3-inch guns, which overlooked the old wharf where Union soldiers once brought in supplies to Fort Pulaski during the Civil War. This was the new age of forts, which would become known as the Endicott Period fortification system.

As the United States began to rebuild, military leaders addressed the need for a new type of fortification to defend the nation. War with Cuba caused concern, and in 1914 the world would erupt into a war involving all major powers, including the United States. Concrete and steel-framed fortifications replaced the old brick forts along America's coastlines. In 1897, Fort Screven was built on Tybee Island and named in honor of another Revolutionary War soldier, Gen. James Screven (1750–1778), who is buried in Midway, Georgia. (Tybee Historical Society.)

Following the Spanish-American War, Fort Pulaski and others had become relics of the past. The concrete bunker fortification was now the more effective means of defense, but even it was about to become obsolete with the advent of bombers in the air and more powerful warships at sea. Without a presence of soldiers and maintenance workers, forts began to fall under siege of the natural surroundings. Vegetation began to cover the walls and parade grounds, and alligators, snakes, turtles, deer, and other wildlife began to roam freely throughout the forts. This photograph, taken in 1900, shows the abandonment of Fort Pulaski. (FPNM.)

This aerial view taken around 1924 gives a clear image of the neglect and abandonment of Fort Pulaski. At one time, a house had been built on the terreplein of the southwest corner bastion, as seen here, which served as a residence for the ordnance sergeant who helped oversee the fort and operations of the newly constructed gun emplacements inside the demilune of Fort Pulaski and Battery Hambright during the Spanish-American War. The house was inherited by the Lighthouse Service in 1906 or 1907, just a few years before the Cockspur Lighthouse was decommissioned. The house burned down in 1925 from a lightning strike. Parts of the gorge of the fort were damaged as well. (FPNM.)

This is a unique view of the ordnance sergeant's house on top of Fort Pulaski. The house had been built on top of the fort after a major hurricane swept through in 1891, causing the sea to rise some five feet high across the parade ground. (FPNM.)

Pres. Calvin Coolidge signed a proclamation under the Antiquities Act of 1906, designating Fort Pulaski as a national monument on October 15, 1924. The proclamation declared the entire 20-acre area "comprising the site of the old fortifications which are clearly defined by ditches and embankments" to be a national monument. However, it would be almost 10 years before preservation work would begin on the abandoned historical fort. President Coolidge would die in 1933 before restoration of the fort could begin. (LOC.)

Following the major wars in which the United States had been involved, many of the massive masonry and concrete forts that had once served as important military posts were decommissioned and abandoned. In some circumstances, only a caretaker stood watch at their gates. Fort Pulaski was one of the many grand fortresses that closed. It quickly fell into disrepair, while the area the fort occupied on Cockspur Island became covered with more vegetation and inhabited by more wildlife. Fort Pulaski and other historic military posts had been managed by the US War Department until 1933, when Pres. Franklin D. Roosevelt issued Executive Order 6166 on June 10, 1933, and No. 6228 on July 28, 1933, which transferred all federally managed military historic sites, battlefields, and monuments to the National Parks Service. (FPNM.)

The Civil Works Administration (CWA) was the first to support the restoration of Fort Pulaski. The CWA projects would include removal of undergrowth and finishing a general engineering survey in preparation for the future work of two other agencies: the Civilian Conservation Corps (CCC) and the Public Works Administration (PWA). In 1933, the CCC emerged to assist citizens in getting back to work. The organization's objective was twofold: to conserve natural resources in the United States and to help give young men an opportunity to work. President Roosevelt's New Deal programs had established several new agencies to help provide work for thousands of Americans. The important work achieved by America's young men from 1933 to 1942 has given the United States a wonderful legacy of preserved natural and physical historic resources. Ultimately, the CCC would be distinguished as the single greatest conservation program in the United States. (LOC.)

In May 1934, the National Park Service was given permission to build Camp 460 on the outer perimeter of Fort Pulaski for the workers. Those who came to work were paid $30 per month and were provided this housing for the duration of the restoration of the fort. (FPNM.)

The initial restoration began with foot bridges crossing the virtually nonexistent moat. Once a seven to eight-foot deep encirclement of water around Fort Pulaski, it now was filled with mud and vegetation. It would all have to be removed. (FPNM.)

The interior of Fort Pulaski, where soldiers once stood on parade, played baseball, and of course, scrambled for protection during the heavy bombardment of 1862, had since turned into a forest. (FPNM.)

Another view of the interior of the fort shows the scraggly growth throughout the structure and around the quarters. Window and door frames had rotted out of the brick framework, and brick and mortar had crumbled. (FPNM.)

This photograph is a later view of the preservation efforts being made to restore Fort Pulaski to its former grandeur. Where the Confederate officers and politicians had once been quartered, the cells and wooden doors had fallen into disrepair and, in many cases, broken off the hinges of the framework. (FPNM.)

As a result of the success the men had in digging out the moat, water from the Savannah River flowed into the moat once again in December 1935 after more than 50 years of being blocked from the mud and vegetation. Here, a worker appears to be holding up a turtle he captured. (FPNM.)

The moat project was finally completed, but there was now the process of clearing the trees and other vegetation inside and around the fort. (FPNM.)

A path had to be cut inside the sally port to get into the interior of the fort. Gradually, trees and brush were cleared to reveal the parade ground where both Union and Confederate soldiers once stood. (FPNM.)

The workers first began clearing the heavy overgrowth that had consumed the fort for more than 30 years. Next, they built trails and roadways to bring heavier equipment closer to the fort so they could begin the process of digging out the moat, rebuilding the drainage systems, and ultimately restoring the fort's interior. Here, workers dig out areas of the parade ground. (FPNM.)

Gradually, the interior of the fort began to take shape once again, although trees and scrub brush still remained throughout the parade ground and around the gun emplacements on the parapet. (FPNM.)

Partial rebuilding and repointing of the brickwork was necessary to restore the stability of the fort after years of the elements causing the bricks to separate and break apart. (FPNM.)

The sally port entrance to the fort had two sets of massive wooden doors on the exterior and the interior. They were painted green, which was a standard color for military structures and equipment. This door actually suffered damage in the upper right corner from the bombardment of 1862. Amazingly, the doors and their original paint have survived throughout history. (FPNM.)

This view from on top of the parapet shows how much vegetation had been cleared from inside the fort by the CCC workers. Some trees and bushes appear to be left for decorative purposes, but most would ultimately be removed to bring the fort back to virtually its original appearance as an early US military post. (FPNM.)

As the fort was being preserved, the National Park Service staff began seeking opportunities to acquire cannon to put on the walls of the fort to add to its prominence as a National Historic Landmark. In 1939, the NPS purchased this double-banded Brooke rifle, once part of the defenses of Savannah during the Civil War, for just $50 from the Knight Scrap Iron Company. These guns await installation on the terreplein of Fort Pulaski. The Brooke gun alone weighs 10,200 pounds. (FPNM.)

Pictured here in 1939, a park ranger stands smiling at the newly preserved Fort Pulaski. (FPNM.)

The National Park Service, founded in 1916, has preserved our historic and natural landmarks for almost a century. (FPNM.)

Fort Pulaski was rebuilt by Union troops following the bombardment in 1862. However, more work had to be done to preserve and stabilize the walls when the fort was closed and abandoned following the Civil War and Spanish-American War. (FPNM.)

This is one of the first official permanent entrance signs to Fort Pulaski. It cost 25¢ for adults and was free for children 12 years or under. This photograph was taken in March 1964. (FPNM.)

Today, the walls still hold together in spite of the massive bombardment of the Union forces in April 1862 and the lengthy period of neglect. It is a testament to the craftsmanship of the men who originally built this mighty structure. (FPNM.)

The 48th New York State Volunteers, Company F, reactivated, is part of the many living historians who bring Fort Pulaski to life throughout the year with interpretive programs that help visitors better visualize and understand the life of the Civil War soldiers who lived, marched, and stood guard inside these walls. (Mark Avery.)

The 48th New York State Volunteers, Company F, reactivated, comes to Fort Pulaski each Veterans Day weekend to recreate the life of the Union soldiers who garrisoned the fort during the American Civil War. This 2013 Garrison Weekend shows how popular this national landmark has become to interested visitors.

In 2013, the 48th New York State Volunteers, Company F, reactivated, had a unique experience in recreating the artillery drill, which the regiment performed regularly under the supervision and instruction of the 3rd Rhode Island Artillery more than 150 years ago. Pictured here from right to left are Joe Blunt, Ken Giddens, Shawn Butler, an unidentified park ranger, Mike Wood (21st Ohio Infantry), and Brian Smith (1st New York Engineers) manning this 30-pound Parrott rifle gun.

Historically, the 48th New York State Volunteer Infantry played baseball during their time at Fort Pulaski. Here, member Jeff Kirkland, son of retired park ranger Talley Kirkland, poses in casual attire ready for a game.

The 48th New York State Volunteer Infantry, reactivated, plays a game of baseball on the parade ground inside Fort Pulaski as the original soldiers did in 1862.

The 48th New York State Volunteers, Company F, reactivated, stands on parade as they did more than 150 years ago. (Joel Cadoff, FPNM.)

The 48th New York State Volunteers, Company F, reactivated, marches out of Fort Pulaski, concluding another Garrison Weekend living history program. The reenactment group continues a good working relationship with the National Park Service in preserving and sharing the history of this grand fort and the men and women who have served within its walls. The unit has been coming to Fort Pulaski since 1989. (Mark Avery.)

Talley Kirkland, retired park ranger, and Joel Cadoff, park ranger, pose for a unique photograph of two generations of dedicated national park rangers of Fort Pulaski.

Joel Cadoff continues the tradition of his predecessor, Talley Kirkland, with the announcement on top of the fort: "Fort Pulaski is now closed."

Fort Pulaski National Monument continues to remain strong after more than 165 years since its completion in 1847. Thousands of visitors venture to see this architectural marvel of a military age of long ago. (FPNM.)

The sun sets on yet another day of this grand military architectural masterpiece. Fort Pulaski National Monument continues to stand firm after more than 165 years of weathering the natural elements, gunfire piercing its walls, and visitors climbing its ramparts daily. This mighty fortress is a tribute to the American soldier and a fine example of the investment and commitment our forefathers made to defend the United States of America. (Joel Cadoff, FPNM.)

# BIBLIOGRAPHY

Carse, Robert. *Department of the South: Hilton Head in the Civil War.* Columbia, SC: The State Printing Company, 1961.

Gilmore, Quincy. *Siege and Reduction of Fort Pulaski.* New York: Dan Van Nostrand, 1862. Reprinted by Thomas Publications, 1988.

Guss, John Walker. *Fortresses of Savannah Georgia.* Charleston, SC: Arcadia Publishing, 2002.

Lattimore, Ralston B. *Fort Pulaski National Monument.* Washington, DC: US Government Printing Office, 1954 (Reprint 1961).

Lee, Robert E. *Robert E. Lee, Recollections and Letters.* New York: Doubleday, Page & Company, 1904.

McMurry, Richard M. *Footprints of a Regiment, A Recollection of the 1st Georgia Regulars, 1861–1865, 1st Sergeant W.H. Andrews.* Marietta, GA: Longstreet Press, 1992.

Palmer, Abraham J. *The History of the Forty-Eighth Regiment New York State Volunteers.* Brooklyn, NY: Veteran Association of the Regiment, 1885.

Schiller, Herbert M. *Sumter Is Avenged: The Siege and Reduction of Fort Pulaski.* Shippensburg, PA: White Maine Publishing Company, 1995.

Trimble, Richard. *Brothers 'Til Death, The Civil War Letter of William, Thomas, and Maggie Jones, 1861–1865.* Macon, GA: Mercer University Press, 2000.

*The War of the Rebellion: A Compilation of the Official Records of the Union and Confederate Armies.* Series 1. Washington, DC: Government Printing Office, 1880–1901.

# INDEX

# DISCOVER THOUSANDS OF LOCAL HISTORY BOOKS FEATURING MILLIONS OF VINTAGE IMAGES

Arcadia Publishing, the leading local history publisher in the United States, is committed to making history accessible and meaningful through publishing books that celebrate and preserve the heritage of America's people and places.

## Find more books like this at
## www.arcadiapublishing.com

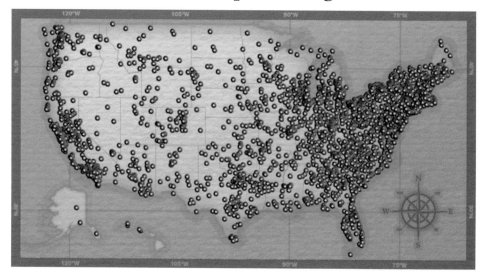

Search for your hometown history, your old stomping grounds, and even your favorite sports team.